RUSSELL WILSON
and the
Seahawks

PAST and PRESENT

BY
ANTHONY CURCIO

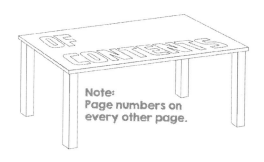

Note:
Page numbers on
every other page.

current players   1

past players   13

design center   31

Then and Now   36

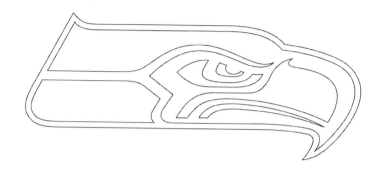

CURRENT PLAYERS

1

Voted a captain in 2014 and helped lead the team to consecutive Super Bowl's. Helped Seattle's defense lead the NFL in scoring for three straight seasons and lead the NFL in both scoring and yards allowed for a second-straight season.

In Super Bowl XLVIII totalled nine tackles, an interception and two passes defensed.

One of the hardest hitters in team history. Puts the "boom" in the Legion of Boom.

12TH

2

Led team in receptions in 2011 (51), 2014 (66) and 2015 (78).

12TH

2015 Season receiving stats:
78 catches, 1069 yards, 14 TD's

3

Sherman's rise to the starting lineup in 2011 truly kicked off the Legion of Boom era. His tip of Colin Kaepernick's pass against the 49ers in the 2014 NFC title game may be the most memorable play in team history.

Since 2011, leads the league in interceptions (26).

25 RICHARD SHERMAN

12TH

Best corner in team history.

4

Jermaine caught the game-winning 35-yard touchdown pass in overtime vs. Green Bay to send Seattle to Super Bowl XLIX and made one of the best catches in Super Bowl history on a 33-yard juggling catch late in the game.

Had 49 catches for 685 yards and 5 touchdowns in 2015.

12TH

Grew up 30 miles from CenturyLink.

5

Voted to four consecutive Pro Bowl's and three consecutive Associated Press First-Team All-Pro's. Thomas and Richard Sherman were the fourth and fifth players to earn back-to-back first-team All-Pro honors in franchise history.

Had 5 interceptions in 2015.

29 EARL THOMAS

12TH

All-Pro First-Team Free Safety

6

Lockett had 51 Catches, 664 Yards and 6 Touchdowns in 2015 season.

12ᵀᴴ

All-Pro Return Man

7

Through game 6 of the 2016 season, Michael has 406 yards and 4 touchdowns.

33 CHRISTINE MICHAEL

12TH

In 2009, Christine won the Walter Payton trophy
for the best high school player in the nation.

8

Great addition to Seattle roster. Acquired from New Orleans. Was the Saints all-time receiving leader by a tight end, started 50 of 78 career games for New Orleans from 2010-14 totaling 386 receptions for 4,752 yards and 51 TDs.
Led the Saints in receptions four consecutive seasons from 2011-14

Graham is second all-time for most receiving yards and touchdowns by a tight end in a single season!

9

Started all 16 games in 2014,
completing 285 of 452 passes (63.1%)
for 3,475 yards, a passer rating of 95.0,
20 touchdowns and seven interceptions.
Also set career-high in rushes (118),
rushing yards (849) and rushing touchdowns (six).

Started all 16 games in 2015,
completing 329 of 483 passes (68.1%)
for 4,024 yards, a passer rating of 110.1,
34 touchdowns and eight interceptions.

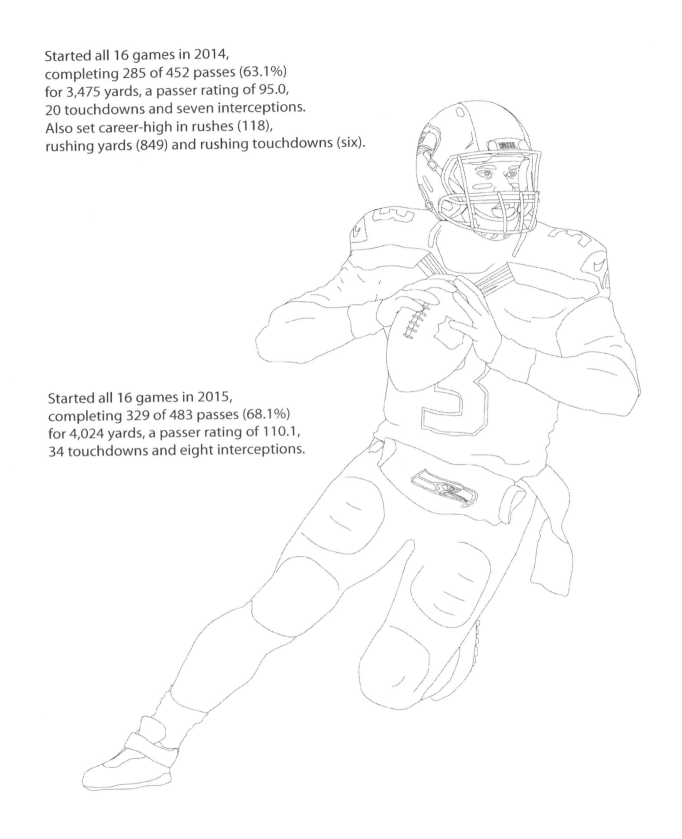

12 TH

The leader of it all.

114 Tackles in 2015. In 2014, Wagner had 104 tackles (67 solo), 2 sacks and three passes defensed and was voted to his first Pro Bowl, in addition to being selected Associated Press First-Team All-Pro.

54 BOBBY WAGNER

12TH

All-Pro First-Team Linebacker.

11

Totalled 44 touchdowns and a career-low 21 interceptions during 2015 season, leading the Hawks in both categories. All passes caught by young fans before official game start.

O BLITZ

The bird. The myth. The legend.

12TH

12

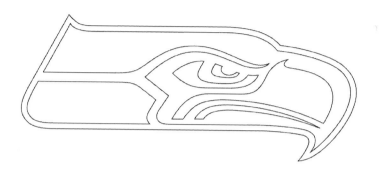

PAST PLAYERS

13

12ᵀᴴ

Played 1990-97. All-Pro RB. Big back 6'2"
Best Season = 1,346 yds, 15 TD's (1995)

14

24 MARSHAWN LYNCH

12TH

BEAST MODE... Played 2010-2015.
Heart and soul of first ever Super Bowl team.

15

12 TH

16

Hawks All-Pro strong safety from 1981-87.
NFL Defensive Player of the Year 1984 (w/10 int)

12TH

Speedy WR and return man played for SEA '95-'99.
4 punt return touchdowns are franchise record.

17

1 WARREN MOON

12TH

Hall of fame player who played for Hawks
near end of his career (as did Jerry Rice).

18

12TH

**Played with Hawks from 1983-89. All-Pro RB
Rookie season had 1,449 yds and 13 TD's.**

19

96 CORTEZ KENNEDY

12TH

**Hawks defensive tackle from 1990-2000.
NFL Defensive Player of Year (1992)**

20

10 JIM ZORN

12TH

**Hawks QB from 1976-84.
Very first quarterback the Hawks ever had!**

21

12TH

**Hawks RB from 2000-07.
SEA records in rushing yards and TD's**

22

12ᵀᴴ

23

Hawks receiver from 1988-98.
2nd in career catches and receiving yards.

22 DAVE BROWN

12 TH

24

Hawks cornerback from 1976-86.
SEA records for most INT (50) and INT TD's (5).

8 MATT HASSELBECK

12TH

Hawks QB from 2001-2010.
First QB to lead SEA to Super Bowl.

25

12TH

Hawks Defensive End from 1980-91.
SEA records in career sacks (116).

12TH

Hawks corner from 1997-2003.
2 interceptions for TD's in second year.

27

17 DAVE KRIEG

12TH

Played QB for Hawks from 1980-91.
SEA record for most career TD passes (195).

28

12TH

**Hawks Left Tackle from 1997-2009.
One of the best left tackles in NFL history.**

29

80 STEVE LARGENT

12TH

**Played receiver for Hawks from 1976-1989.
One of the greatest receivers in NFL history.**

30

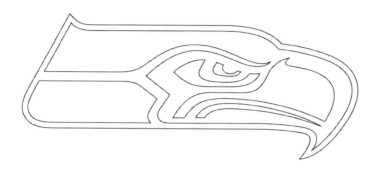

DESIGN CENTER

It's time to design the new Seahawks, let's start with the logo!

32

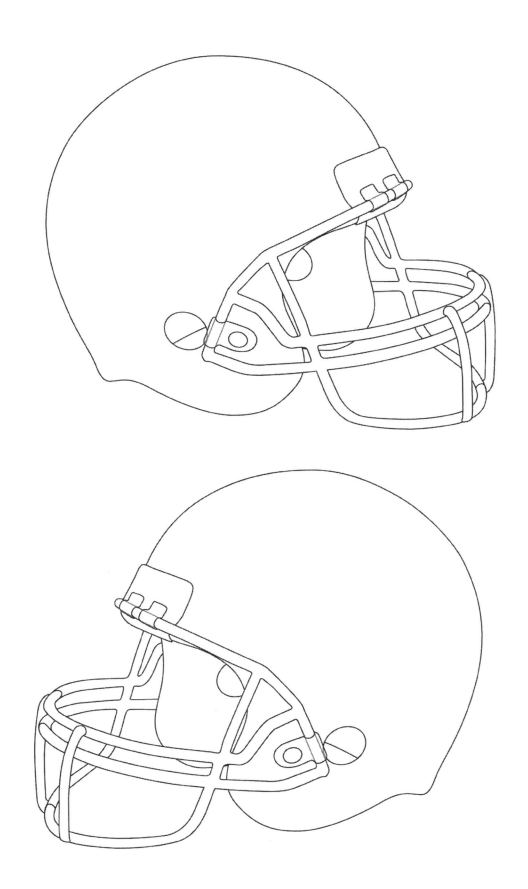

**Next...
The helmets.**

33

And finally, the whole uniform!

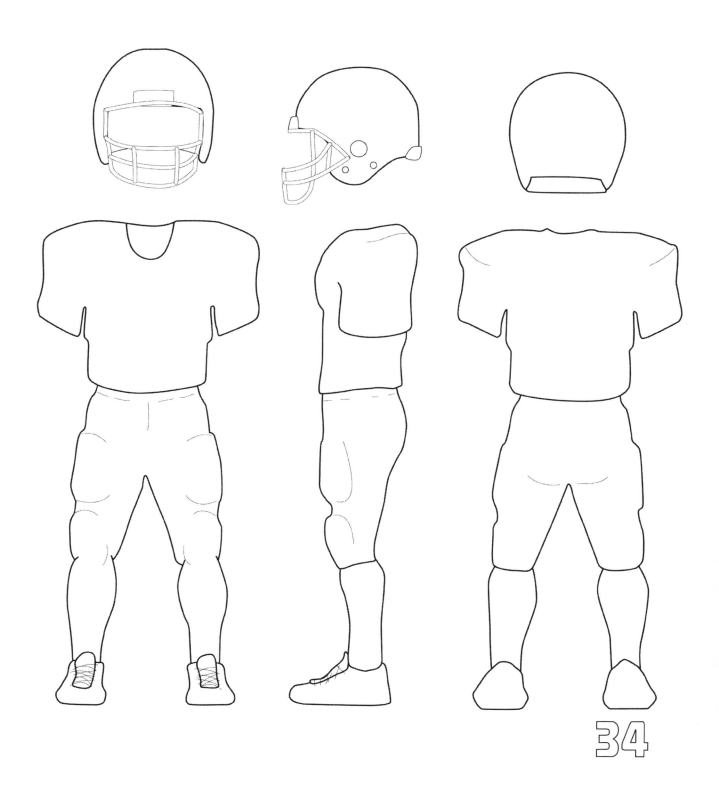

34

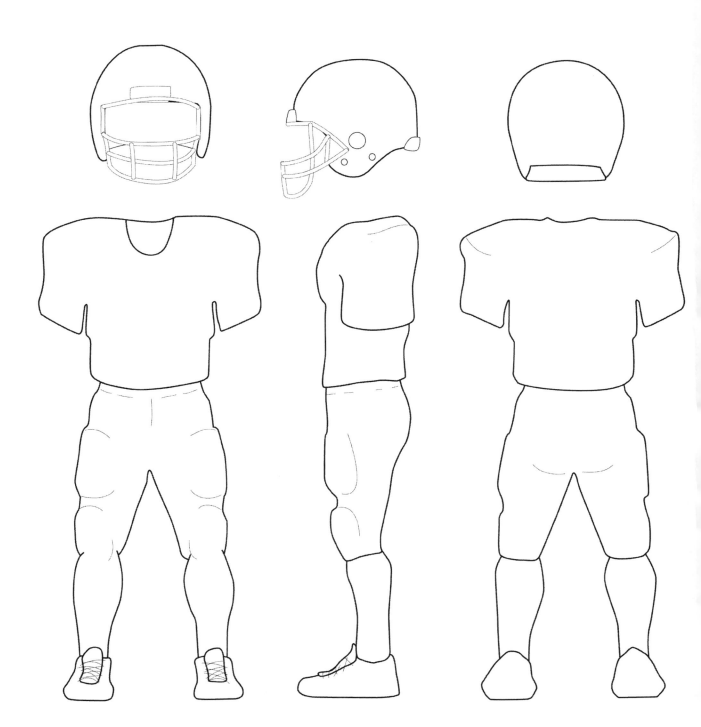

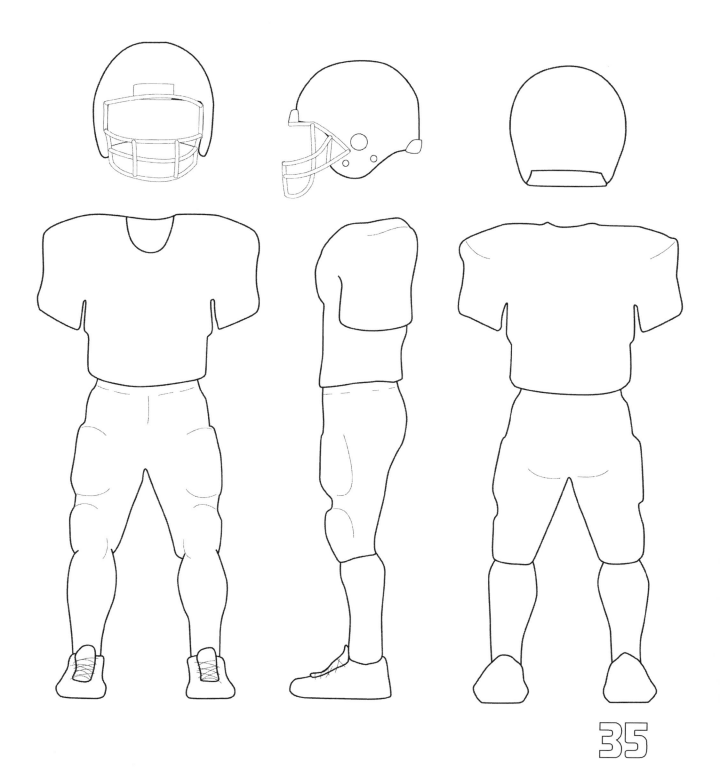

35

Seahawks uniform changes over time.

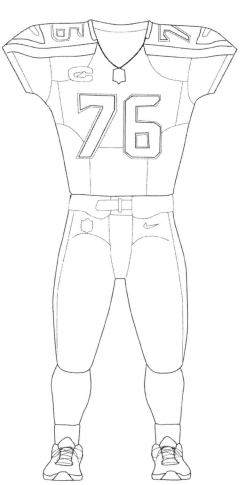

1976

NOW

36

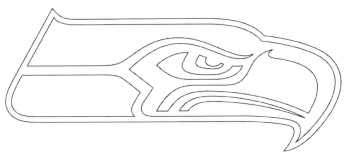

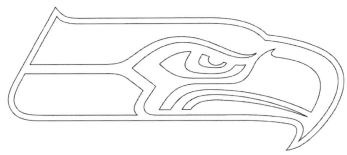

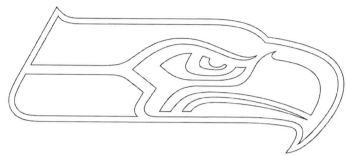

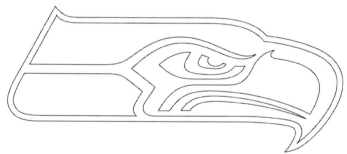

37

Made in the USA
Columbia, SC
13 November 2020